WILLIAMSBURG VIRGINIA

A Brief Study in Photographs

WILLIAMSBURG:
Published by *COLONIAL WILLIAMSBURG*, Incorporated
MCMXL

FIRST PRINTING 1939
SECOND PRINTING REVISED 1940

COPYRIGHT 1940 · COLONIAL WILLIAMSBURG, INC., WILLIAMSBURG, VA.

CONTENTS

    I. PREFACE   9

   II. INTRODUCTION   11

  III. THE WREN BUILDING of the COLLEGE:

        Its Principal Facade   17
        The Chapel   19
        The West Elevation   21

  IV. THE COLONIAL CAPITOL:

        Its West and South Fronts   23
        The Hall of the House of Burgesses   25
        The Council Chamber   27
        The Room for the General Court   29

   V. THE PUBLIC GAOL:

        The North Elevation   31
        A Criminal Cell   33
        The Pillory   35

VI. THE GOVERNOR'S PALACE:

The Principal Front	37
The Great Stair	39
The Parlor	41
The Outside Kitchen	43
The Little Middle Room	45
The Supper Room	47
The Ball Room Wing	49

VII. BRUTON PARISH CHURCH:

A View from the Street	51
An Interior View	53

VIII. THE PUBLIC MAGAZINE:

An Exterior View	55

IX. THE LUDWELL-PARADISE HOUSE:

Looking Past the Apothecary Shop	57
The Stable and Coach House	59

X. THE RALEIGH TAVERN:

The Main Entrance	61
The Parlor	63

X. THE RALEIGH TAVERN (Continued):

    The Bar   65

    "The Apollo"   67

XI. THE GEORGE WYTHE HOUSE:

    A View from the Palace Green   69

    The Parlor   71

XII. A SMALL RESIDENCE and GARDEN:

    The Galt Cottage   73

XIII. THE COURT HOUSE of 1770:

    A View from the Market Square   75

XIV. MEN WORKING:

    The Cabinet Maker   77

    The Blacksmith   79

    The Wig Maker   81

XV. THE MARKET SQUARE TAVERN:

    Rear View from the Garden   83

XVI. THE WILLOW TREE   85

PREFACE

THE restoration of Williamsburg, second capital of Virginia, to its colonial appearance was begun in 1927 and is still in progress. In the course of these years the undertaking has become one of the major educational endeavors ever to be attempted in this country.

The Restoration is a composite representation of an important period of English-American colonial history, rather than of a given time within that period. It represents the whole span of urban life in the largest and most powerful of the English colonies in the eighteenth century; yet, because of the city's unusual nature, the Restoration bespeaks the life of the entire colony of which Williamsburg was the seat of government from 1699 through 1779. For example, the discrepancy between the city's size and its importance is in itself remindful of Virginia's plantation civilization—a system so pronounced that large cities and towns could not be created, despite the constant efforts and encouragements of officials at home and abroad. On the other hand, the simple magnificence of so small a city was and is indicative of the opulence and culture which pervaded the Virginia colony.

The fields of interest which restored Williamsburg embraces are many and varied. Architecture, decoration, the arts and crafts, horticulture, and scholarly pursuits are all involved, both in their English antecedents and in their American adaptation or development. The Restoration, while exemplifying each, is devoted exclusively to none, but affords a blending of them all in a broad historical presentation. Visual interpretation, moreover, is bringing about an increasing awareness of many of the intangible qualities of the colonial period which otherwise could not be attained. These qualities go far in making the period in question worthy of recalling.

In this book an effort is made to offer a highly condensed pictorial indication of the inspiration and instruction which the restored city may afford its visitors through centuries to come.

COLONIAL WILLIAMSBURG, *Incorporated*.

Williamsburg, Virginia
August, 1939.

INTRODUCTION

WILLIAMSBURG had its beginnings in what was known as "the Middle Plantation," lying between small tributaries of the York and James rivers. Specifically, Middle Plantation was probably the central point on a ridge of land at the middle of the palisades which protected the lower Virginia peninsula from the incursions of the Indians.

Through the seventeenth century it grew gradually in size and importance. It is probable that at first it was a place of gathering for those who inhabited the open lands maintained along the palisades. In time, in an expanding colony, it came to be looked upon as a place more safe and central than Jamestown. At the time of Bacon's memorable Rebellion in 1676, Middle Plantation served as a center of Baconian activities, and was mentioned as "the very heart and centre of the country."

Through the destruction of Jamestown, Bacon's Rebellion hastened the rise of Middle Plantation. In 1699, though a none too successful endeavor had been made to rehabilitate Jamestown, the General Assembly of Virginia passed an act, entitled "An act directing the building the Capitoll and the City of Williamsburg," which gave detailed instructions for the establishment of the capital at "the place commonly called and known by the name of the Middle Plantation." This act directed that the new city be named Williamsburg in honor of William III.

Unlike many colonial cities which developed more or less at random, Williamsburg was ordered and laid out in accordance with a general plan, beyond the bounds of which it never grew. Indeed, the city did not ever fulfill the modest hopes and plans of those who visualized a city in Virginia; for, though incorporated as a city in 1722, its resident colonial population never exceeded two thousand persons.

At normal seasons of the year the city placidly engaged in its routine occupations as a center of government and as the seat of the College of William and Mary, which had been established at Middle Plantation in 1693. Tradesmen and craftsmen, while serving the needs of its small population and those of occasional visitors from the plantations, laid by their wares against the "Public Times" which gave to Williamsburg another aspect.

Public Times, occurring whenever the General Assembly convened and the courts sat at Williamsburg, usually in the Spring and Fall, gave rise to a social phenomenon which was not duplicated elsewhere in the colonies. Affairs of every description were regulated to fall at these times, and on these occasions Williamsburg became a veritable metropolis. Its population increased two and three times its normal size and continued thus enlarged so long as the Assembly stood convened. The agricultural nature of the colony and the pronounced scarcity of towns and cities tended to center the social structure of Virginia at Williamsburg. In so far as this condition was unusual in the colonies, to that same degree was Williamsburg unique among the colonial capitals. In it is found an explanation of the prominence which Williamsburg enjoyed and enjoys today.

In other words, in view of the fact that it was a periodic clearing house in matters of government, politics, business, religion, social obligations, and entertainment for a diffused population, Williamsburg shared more intimately than most colonial capitals in the life of the colony at large. Here were weighed and directed the Virginia activities in the French and Indian War. Here were compounded and from here disseminated the Virginia influences in the cause of independence and the War of the Revolution. Here were formulated many of the principles of democratic government.

These same conditions also explain the nineteenth and early twentieth century history of Williamsburg; for, upon the removal of the seat of government to Richmond in 1779, the city was left with the attitudes and appurtenances of an important past, though its activities centered around an impoverished college and the functions of a small county seat.

A century and a half of inactivity, interrupted only by the War Between the States and the World War, had left pronounced marks on the city when its restoration was begun. Yet this same inactivity was responsible for the fact that Williamsburg retained a large proportion of its colonial buildings. In 1927, through the influence of the Reverend Dr. William A. R. Goodwin, rector of Bruton Parish Church, Mr. John D. Rockefeller, Jr., became interested in and undertook the restoration.

Since that time 586 modern buildings have been demolished; 72 colonial buildings have been restored; 176 buildings have been reconstructed upon carefully excavated colonial foundations. Certain of the restored buildings have been returned to their original uses. Others have been completely refurnished, as far as possible in accordance with colonial inventories, and opened as exhibition buildings. The majority of the restored and reconstructed residences are privately tenanted, in order that the colonial area may continue alive. Carefully restored gardens are to be seen on every hand, and craftsmen are again at work in ancient or reconstructed shops. Other buildings and gardens will be added from time to time, until exhibition buildings exemplifying the social order and the types of commercial activity in Williamsburg in the eighteenth century are provided.

From such scenes the following photographs are selected. In view of the fact that an extensive presentation cannot be accomplished in a book of this size, the majority of the pictures portray buildings and grounds which are open for public inspection.

—*Rutherfoord Goodwin.*

THE PHOTOGRAPHS
by Richard Garrison

THE Great Building of the College of William and Mary was erected at Middle Plantation in 1695-98 from plans prepared by Sir Christopher Wren. It is the oldest academic building standing in the United States.

THE Chapel wing was added to the Wren Building of the College in 1732. Lord Botetourt, Sir John Randolph, Peyton Randolph, and John Randolph, "the Tory," are buried in vaults beneath the chancel floor.

THE west elevation of the Wren Building of the College includes two wings, the Great Hall and the Chapel, which were to have formed two sides of the quadrangle originally intended, but never completed.

*T*HE *Capitol, ordered built in 1699, succeeded the State Houses of Jamestown. It burned in 1747, was rebuilt, and served until Richmond became the capital in 1780. Destroyed in 1832, it was rebuilt in 1930-34.*

THE Hall of the House of Burgesses, the lower house of the General Assembly, was the scene of legislative procedure and much of the revolutionary activity of the colony and Commonwealth from 1704 to 1780.

*T*HE *Governor and the Council, the upper house of the General Assembly, performed their executive and legislative functions in the Council Chamber of the Capitol. Its furnishings were specified by the Assembly.*

*T*HE Governor and Council performed their judicial functions as "The General Court," the highest court of the Colony. Here they served as a court of appeals and, in certain cases, as a court of original jurisdiction.

*T*HE Public Gaol confined principally those brought from county gaols for trial in the General Court. Fifteen followers of "Blackbeard," the pirate, were imprisoned here in 1718. Cells were provided for debtors.

CRUDE *sanitary facilities and unglazed windows added to the discomfort of the shackled prisoners in criminal cells. The food slot is a survival from the original gaol of 1701, which was altered from time to time.*

*P*RISONERS *were rarely punished by long confinement in the Public Gaol. Quick punishments were imposed on those convicted in the General Court. In the Pillory lesser offenders were pelted by the populace.*

ERECTED in 1706-20, the Governor's Palace was the home of seven governors for the Crown and the first two governors of the Commonwealth. The Palace was reconstructed in 1930-34, it having burned in 1781.

As an estate, the Palace was reputed "the best in all the English America . . . exceeded by few . . . in England." The reconstructed stairway is in keeping with contemporary Virginia and English precedent.

Accurately costumed hostesses and attendants interpret and maintain the exhibition buildings. The Palace parlor is furnished in keeping with the inventories of colonial occupants, as are its other rooms.

Royal governors complained that the demands of Virginia hospitality impoverished them. On occasion meals for two hundred guests were prepared in the outside kitchen and carried to the Palace in covered dishes.

*I*N *the Little Middle Room food from the kitchen was warmed and served to the three dining rooms of the Palace. Several Delft tiles of the fireplace facing were found in excavating the original foundations.*

THE Supper Room, which adjoins the ballroom, is furnished with period antiques and is papered with eighteenth century Chinese wallpaper. This room provides a striking example of Chippendale influence.

THE Ball Room wing, opening on a formal garden, was added to the Palace about 1752, at a time when newly erected plantation houses in Virginia had begun to challenge the magnificence of the governor's home.

*B*RUTON *Parish Church, called "the Court Church of colonial Virginia," was completed in 1715. Most colonial Virginians of prominence attended services here, and many are buried in its aisles and churchyard.*

*A*N *eighteenth century pipe organ again looks down from the organ loft on the panelled pulpit and canopied governor's pew in the restored interior of the Church. Aisles and chancel floor are of English stone.*

THE Assembly, in 1714, authorized the building of a Magazine for the Colony's arms. Confiscation of the powder from this Magazine in 1775 precipitated the Revolution in Virginia. It was restored in 1935.

*D*R. *Archibald Blair's Apothecary Shop stood near the town house of the Ludwells. The eccentric Lucy Ludwell Paradise once occupied the latter. Both of these eighteenth century buildings have been restored.*

WHEN the Ludwell-Paradise House was advertised for rent in the 18th century, its stable was mentioned as an important asset. Reconstructed in 1931, the building now shelters coach horses and two colonial vehicles.

*A*MONG colonial taverns, the Raleigh was notable as a social, political, and commercial center. In Virginia it ranked next to the Capitol as a scene of Revolutionary activity. Burned in 1859, it was reconstructed in 1932.

*T*HE *prestige of the Raleigh Tavern and the detailed inventories of two of its colonial keepers served as a guide in refurnishing it. Lafayette was entertained here, and his portrait hangs above the mantel in the Parlor.*

*B*ARGAINS *were sealed and history made in the Bar of the Raleigh. Here colonial patriots agreed to drink no tea. The Bar is protected by a wicket, behind which a trap door leads down to the wine cellar.*

In "the Apollo," the principal room of the Raleigh, the Phi Beta Kappa Society is believed to have been founded. Prior to the Revolution, the Burgesses met here as conventions when dissolved by royal governors.

THE George Wythe House, home of a signer of the Declaration of Independence, is representative of the more elaborate colonial city residences. Washington and Rochambeau had revolutionary headquarters here.

THE furnishings of the Wythe House are reminiscent of the last quarter of the eighteenth century. It is believed that the interior walls of the parlor were whitewashed, as were the majority in Williamsburg.

A FEW old buildings have been moved into the restored area to replace missing 18th century structures. The James Galt Cottage, here seen from the adjoining garden, exemplifies this type of restoration.

*T*HE *city and county Court House, erected in 1770, occupied the center of the Market Square. It replaced an earlier court house which stood nearby. It was restored in 1932, having been damaged by fire in 1911.*

*C*RAFTSMEN, *often working with 18th century tools, are again employed at ancient trades in the restored and reconstructed shops. This cabinetmaker reproduces and repairs the work of his colonial predecessors.*

A BLACKSMITH *operates the reconstructed smithy of Elkanah Deane, coachmaker and protege of Lord Dunmore. Most other crafts depended upon blacksmiths, who were often men of some consequence.*

A PERUKE maker again pursues his ancient trade in one of the restored shops. Wig-makers were often barbers, and barbers were sometimes surgeons. The wig-maker here gives the finishing touches to a wig.

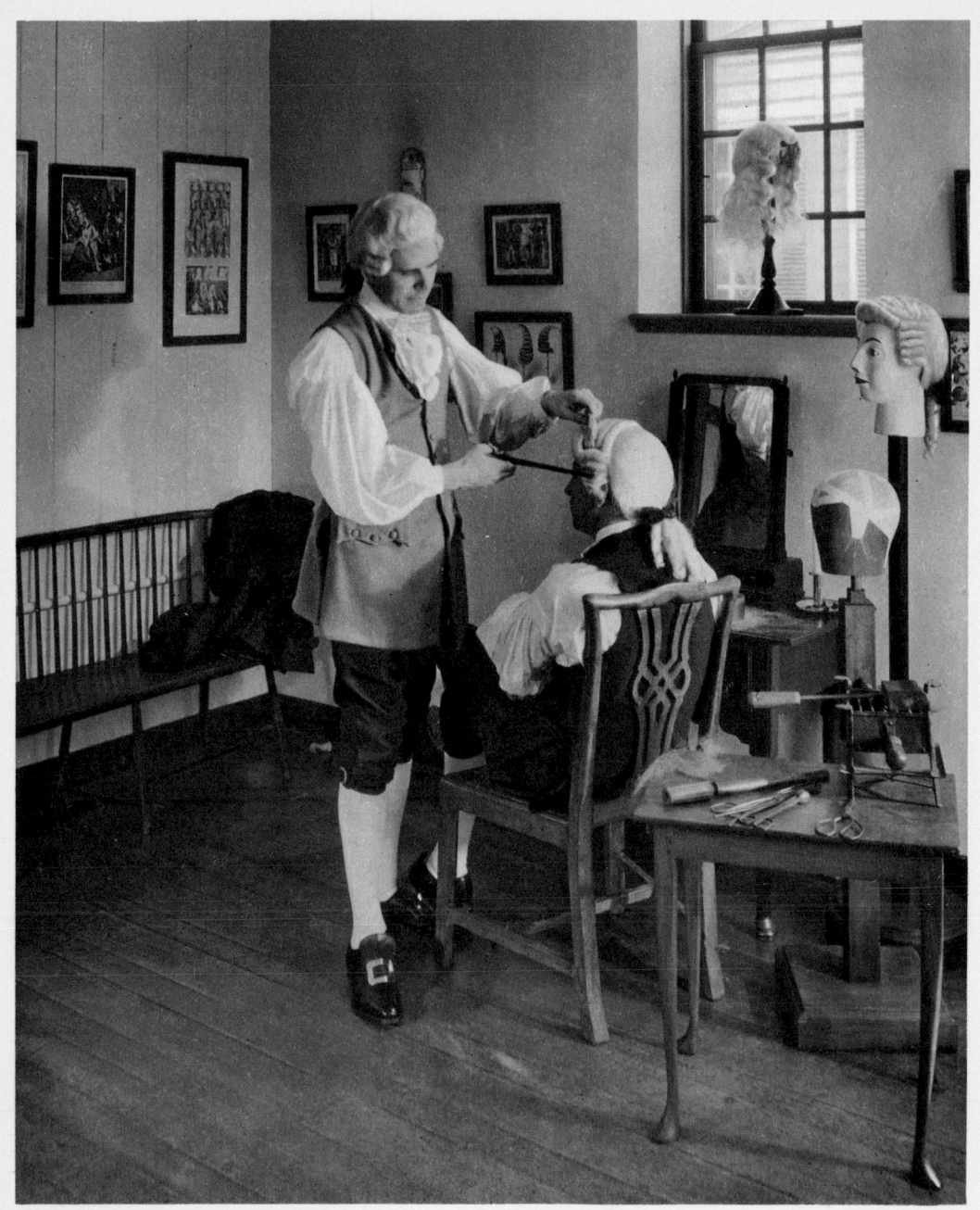

*T*HE Market Square Tavern was first operated as a tavern about 1770. Its kitchen, with servants quarters above, is characteristic of Virginia outbuildings. The tavern was often altered and is now restored.

ONE hundred and fifty-six American soldiers were buried in the Palace garden in 1781 while that building served as a hospital during the Siege of Yorktown. Like Williamsburg, they were for a time forgotten.

WHITTET & SHEPPERSON, PRINTERS, RICHMOND, VA.